SAME NIGHT SEX SYSTEM!

THOTH/ROCHELLE
Publications

THOTH/ROCHELLE PUBLICATIONS
Los Angeles, California

Copyright 2009 by Vince Kelvin, LASEC. All rights reserved worldwide.

Cover and Book Design: Amy M. Kelvin.

Published and distributed by Thoth/Rochelle Publications.

Photos by iStockphoto.com

Special thanks to Larry D. and Seva aka SMERSH, for their assistance with proofreading.

No part of this book may be reproduced or distributed in any form or by any means. Including but not limited to, mechanical, photographic, electronic, or phonographic process. Nor may it be stored in any retrieval systems, transmitted, or otherwise be copied for public or private use without the written permission of the author and publisher.

The information contained in this book is designed for fully functional matured adults over 18 years of age only! The author is simply sharing options that are in no way a substitute for professional mental, emotional and physical care. As the reader, you assume full responsibility for yourself and anyone involved and concerned for any result or consequence whatsoever.

Only read forward if you understand and accept these terms and are 100% committed to ONLY practice safe, mutually consensual, and healthy sex.

ISBN 978-0-578-04929-8

Printed in the United States of America

* Contents *

Foreword_____vii

Introduction_____ix

How to Best Benefit from this Book_____xiii

CHAPTER

I: *What It Really Takes to Have Sex With Women You Just Met*_____3

II: *S = Selection: Spot the Slut, Logistic Friendly Location and Situations that Are Conducive to Sex*_____9

III: *A = Anticipate, Assume, Adventure Frame*_____15

IV: *M = Middle Ground - Finding Your SEXUAL EQUILIBRIUM*_____21

V: *E = Evoke Her Sexual Side*_____25

VI: *N = Negation - Matching and Leading the Natural Female Permission Model*_____29

VII: *I = Information Gathering - The "5 Ps" Elicitation Questions*_____33

VIII: *G = Games and Role Play for SEXUAL CONDUCTIVITY*_____39

IX: *H = Hierarchy - How to Find the One Step She'll Take for Sure*_____43

X: *T = Time Focus - Triggering the "Fuck It, I Want This Now" Mind Set*_____47

XI: *S = Sexual Frames - Reasons to Justify Sexual Actions*_____51

XII: *E = Escalating Sexually - Get Passed The Panties*_____55

XIII:	*X = The X-tra Ingredient - How to Tap Into Divine Pussy Providence*	61
XIV:	*Step 1: Sexual Leadership - It's Not Going to Suck Itself*	67
XV:	*Step 2: Sexual Screening - If She Doesn't Like It Now, She Won't Later*	69
XVI:	*Step 3: Sexual Tension - Dual Direction Game ™*	73
XVII:	*Step 4: Sexual and Sub-Sexual Themes - Making Every Topic Arousing*	77
XVIII:	*Step 5: Sexual Interest - When and How to Tell Her You Want Her*	81
XIX:	*Step 6: Sexual Elicitation - Awaken the Slut Within*	85
XX:	*Step 7: Sequential Seduction - Secrets of Sexual Conditioning*	89
XI:	*Sexual Surrender: When to Just Shut Up and Take Her*	95
XII:	*NMS = Next Morning SEX*	97
Conclusion		99

APPENDIX

Your Bonus Complimentary Training	103
Recommended Resources	104
About the Author	107

✴ ✴ ✴

To every men on the planet
whose enthusiasm for life has been affected
by sexual frustration and starvation.

May their awakening to new
healthier sexual options, solutions,
and possibilities rekindle their soul and spirit!

Remember...

SAFE SEX
OR NO SEX!

✴ ✴ ✴

✳ Foreword ✳

In all the midst of pickup and dating products offering hope and promises, it's rare that something comes along that rings true from beginning to end without the fluff and hype.

A few years back, Vince took me through an adventure that forever changed my perceptions of what I thought reality was. We claimed Hollywood as our refuge, and I endured what were probably the most grueling 14 days of my life. Approaching women from 6pm to 2am every night. There's a reason why I drove out to see him 70 miles each day...he was truly walking the talk!

It didn't take me long to figure out why the Roosevelt Hotel bar/lounge on Hollywood Blvd. was his favorite location...it was all logistics. Though I had only been in the game for a few short months, Vince made me his experiment and vowed that by the time our sessions were over, I would have several lays under my belt.

On day 10 I had already had 2 new "lays" using his methods from girls at work that only a week prior would have nothing to do with me. One of them was a newly married girl. I was convinced! I was sold!

When Vince first told me he was going to write a book on the Same Night Lay subject, I wasn't really sure it could be done. Watching Vince in action and having him demonstrate his "pulls" couldn't be translated into text I thought. I went ahead and read the book, and I couldn't have been more wrong. He somehow managed to take everything he taught me (and thousands of others) and compile it into perhaps the most definitive product ever written on the subject. Not just an instant classic; if you have a set of balls it's almost mandatory you check this out. This is a book every male should read.

*-J the Ripper - **Founder of Casanova Crew***

✴ Introduction ✴

"**P**ut one of those gurus from the Himalayas in an LA night club and tell them to get laid, let's see how enlightened they are!"

- Hypnotica

Why Same Night Sex?

Sex with Hot Girls...

Is for most guys a catch 22! Lack of results has them approach women in such an awkward way or so rarely, it causes women to be repelled! Plunging them further into a loop so viciously limiting, when stuck in it, it seems nearly impossible to even dare to ever envision a reality that meets wild fantasies! Leaving for only options; **sexually settling, struggling, suffering and starving!**

Even for those who are naturally already doing quite well with women, there's always some situations and/or certain women, usually the ones we most desire, which tend to bring out similar challenges, or at least prevent them from being at their best.

Yet regardless of how well or not so well you've been doing up until now, let's discover together how you can begin to uncover your greatest sexual potential and destiny.

Superficial at the Surface, BUT...
ESSENTIAL at the Core!

Yes, some may find the idea of mastering the art of same night sex, rather shallow. But in truth, I personally found that as the above quote from my friend and colleague Hypnotica implies, reaching that place of sexual success took more inner work and lead to greater levels of personal enlightenment, than improving any other aspect of my life! And it's also true that lack of sexual satisfaction is often so detrimental to a man's soul and spirit, that it can deeply affect all other areas.

I've experienced firsthand the impact on self-esteem that "not getting any" can have, as well as how uplifting it can be to regain a sense of sexual choice and possibilities. In my now two decades of assisting others to embrace greater levels of living, I've seen college kids barely starting in life and powerful accomplished men alike being down and depressed, wrestling with how disarming not feeling worthy of great sex with beautiful women can be. Not to mention the indirectly deteriorating effect on the psyche of having to rely solely on pornography and masturbation as a long-term solution!

That is why of all the topics I could have picked; I choose the controversial, yet much needed topic of Same Night Sex. Not intending to encourage men to carelessly get laid, on the contrary, far from that, but to simply strip away all the illusions that prevented you to realize; that of course, you are capable to be fully successful and fulfilled in this area of your life as well.

A Winning Equation for Women Too!

And for women reading this, you already know how challenging it can be to deal with horny guys, LOL! Men who have so little sexual options, they try to get you in bed in ways that are so needy, it becomes creepy! What woman would ever want to be with a guy who's only going for her because he has no other possibilities?

That is why our intention here is to help men rise above "just wanting to get laid", into becoming real romantic heroes and sexual gentlemen who will either sweep you off your feet and finally give you the real sex you've been unconsciously longing for, or leave you alone, because they come from a place of choice and options -- no longer desperation!

And finally, for anyone wondering, "Do I need to have same night sex with the women I meet?" The answer of course is that you only need what is important for you. However you'll enjoy the benefits of this book, find what your true core values and needs are, and honor them, be it in a more casual or committed manner.

So may your manhood radiate on women like warm rays of sun on beautiful flowers to help them more fully blossom! Enjoy the journey, that's where the true rewards are!

**Sexual Sufficiency...
Sexual Freedom....
Sexual Self-Control...
Sexual Enlightenment!**

These are the things we hope this book will bring you, or at least open the door to for you...

Vince Kelvin, and Amy M. Kelvin

How to Best Benefit from this Book:

1. Learning is Like Love Making!

One of the main reasons why average guys tend to not "get some," despite the fact that they may try really hard is that their whole approach to sex is geared towards "getting." They lack a real sense of receptivity, sharing, and giving. They end up alone because they don't think in terms of mutual pleasure and adventure.

This imbalance often shows not only in the way they approach women and life, but also their learning! They want to GET the answer, that secret formula; they are craving the quick fix, but are not willing to give it all they have.

2. These Pages are Not Complete Until You DO YOUR PART!

I've written this book in a unique way in which not only you'll receive incredible information, you will also have to complete the suggested exercises, missions and assignments. That part is entirely up to you, and your choice. Yet knowing the incredible payoff that future sexual adventures will bring you, wouldn't you agree that it would be well worth it to take the time to do all the exercises? It all starts with a small step! No surprise most guys don't get the sex they want, when very few will even want to pick up a pen and start writing! To get, we must give! So give this book all you got so it can give you all you want to get.

3. Overnight Success is a Process!

As much as the concept of practicing through time to get sex on the same night may appear like a contradiction, it reminds me of hearing a famous rock band joke about the fact that they experienced "over-night" success after 20 years of practice, LOL! Now rest assured, it will certainly not take that long, especially when you do your part. Yet how rapidly you'll get results will also depend on what you bring to the plate. While those who already do quite well with women may indeed experience same night sex on their first attempt to apply this material, it may, for others, take a little longer. Regardless, I simply want to encourage you to apply the magic word that guarantees success: UNTIL! Yes, intelligently readjust and refine UNTIL!

4. Have a Higher Purpose!

Not only it is too "average" to make the aim "getting laid," as it is what every guy wants, it also tends to create too much pressure on both sides, and can cause you to come across as too "sleazy." So find a greater reason to go through this book and start to experiment with women. Choose a purpose that will PROPEL YOU FORWARD FAST. For example, do it to fully tap into your potential as a man, to set a new standard in your life, or simply to have fun. Be certain it includes bringing value to the women whom will be involved. Without becoming "the pleaser," of course.

I personally became more successful the day I dropped the idea of trying to "get laid" and instead embraced a more global goal. My higher purpose through my wilder sexual adventures and experimentations: To be the best lover, seducer, and man I could ever be by the time I would find my true love.

✷ ✷ ✷

Section One:

Same Night Sex MINDSET!

How to Properly Set the Sexual Structure From the Start!

What It Really Takes to Have Sex With Women You Just Met!

What does every single straight guy on a night out have in common???

They ALL would love to HAVE SAME NIGHT SEX with SUPER HOT WOMEN!!!

WOULDN'T YOU??? But as you know, it takes more than **JUST** wanting it really badly! That's why in this **BREAKTHROUGH** book I will help you with all that you need to **FINALLY** experience fun and flawless **SEXUAL ADVENTURES ON THE SPOT!**

When it comes to sex with hot women, we can divide men into four categories:

- Those who have given up on the idea and opted for the sad solution of porn or prostitutes!
- Those who endlessly try but struggle and never really succeed!
- The ones who "get lucky" once in a while!
- The few who more consistently thrive with it!

First group: Average frustrated men who have no idea that regardless of how bad it may have been, we can improve anything in life, including being successful at generating fun sexual encounters. These men don't get any action simply because they don't know they can and that there are ways to make it happen.

THE PROBLEM IS THEIR LACK OF AWARENESS OF CAPACITY AND RESOURCES.

Second group: Creepy "pickup guys" who have not fully accepted themselves as they are, even though they still try hard to get laid. Their lack of trust in themselves has them thinking that the only way a woman would ever do it with them is if they can talk and trick her into it, and women sense that.

THE PROBLEM IS THEY LACK SELF-APPROVAL AND A SENSE OF DESERVINGNESS.

Third group: Accidental naturals who get lucky here and there because they feel pretty good about themselves, and socialize rather easily. BUT they often fall short beyond that. Women too have their own insecurities and issues, and so much can happen on the way to the bedroom. Without a plan of action and a skill set to back it up, even those naturally inclined to do pretty well will struggle more often than they will score.

THE PROBLEM IS THEY LACK STRATEGIES AND DIRECTION.

Fourth group: Men that take matters into their own hands. So let's not leave it up to chance! Let's realize that it is possible for you and start to raise your sense of self-approval and deservingness. So together we can come up with a game plan and equip yourself with skills and strategies so potent, other men will wonder how do you MAKE IT HAPPEN?

Most Radical Recipe for Real Results and Superior Sex ASAP!

We're going to play all of our aces and get the odds to work in your favor by combining and integrating the following four ingredients...

1. FOUNDATION: Increase your sense of sexual sufficiency and deservingness which will automatically make your interactions with desirable women much more natural.

2. MINDSET: Most new guys want to know what line or routine will get them laid, but it's more about knowing what to pay attention to, and how to pay attention to it.

3. MECHANICS: We'll also add KNOWING WHAT TO DO. I once remember seeing a t-shirt that said, "IT'S NOT GOING TO SUCK ITSELF." It's true; as much as women love it when it feels like it just happened, they also often are waiting for us to make it happen, and for that it takes skills!

4. MAGICAL INGREDIENT: The power of manifestation! In the end, guys who frequently bed women on the same day they met them are guys who expect that. Now do they expect it because it happens to them, or does it happen to them because they expect it??? It's probably both, so we'll also enhance your sense of sexual positive expectations to bring in an element of DIVINE PUSSY PROVIDENCE, LOL!

I am being silly; Let me actually clarify that our system is geared toward HIGH QUALITY EXPERIENCES WITH FULLY FUNCTIONAL BEAUTIFUL WOMEN FOR MEN WHO TRULY VALUE THEMSELVES, THEIR TIME, AND WOMEN. Because of that, you'll certainly find the steps suggested more sophisticated and perhaps even slightly more complex at first, than other approaches that may focus on screwing low value girls in the...

5 D categories: Drunk, Drugged Out, Dumb, Just Dumped, and Desperate. But you certainly deserve better than that!

Your Roadmap to the Bedroom (Back Seat or Bathroom Will Do Too!)

MINDSET is the roadmap; a series of landmarks to pay attention to, so getting laid is less random and more predictable.

An example of a landmark would be how most women, even when they really want sex, will understandably mention at least once that maybe they shouldn't. Most guys stumble and struggle when that comes up, but knowing how to recognize and embrace such a landmark will allow you to utilize everything a woman may say or do to your own advantage.

To help you do that, let's use an acronym with the words, SAME NIGHT SEX. In which each letter will cover a crucial aspect of SAME NIGHT SEX SUCCESS.

A word of caution: avoid getting overly analytical. These guidelines are to be used in a natural fun way that flows, and allows you to be more present with women.

Nevertheless, do your part and learn and practice this material in a way that makes you grow! Never confuse the natural as a slacker; on the contrary, often things come to us much more naturally after we consciously applied ourselves over and over to attain mastery.

Find a balance that allows you to give it all you got in a way that is natural and pleasant.

There will be a gold nugget and exercise for each key point. Either read once all the way first, then go through the book again, and do each exercise, or read until you've reached the first suggested exercise. Only move on when it is completed, until you've done all the exercises at least once or more. Best may be to do one exercise per day.

However you go about it, don't just read the information. Be the kind of man that will apply it right away. Even if the exercises don't directly lead you to sex, they will help you form habits and take steps that will build your confidence and self-esteem, and then sex will non-linearly follow. Often the simple act of concentrating your efforts and willingly taking steps with a positive attitude is all that it takes to step above average and reach wilder result!

So be smart and do the exercises to be fully prepared, because sexual starvation sucks!

S = Selection: Spot the Slut, Logistic Friendly Location and Situations that Are Conducive to Sex!

Donald Trump once said, in a different context, that to succeed in real estate, you had to do it right from the start and get THE BEST LOCATION, Material, Architect, Contractor, and so on...You probably wonder why use Donald Trump as an example in a book for same night sex? It's because the same advice applies here! For the odds to work for you, we're going to build it right from the ground up.

First: Selection of Location! The most challenging aspect that could come in the way of sleeping with the girl you just met is logistics! Who did she arrive with, is she or someone else driving, how far does she live, how early does she have to get up the next day, and so on. As much as I'll also help you to master your ability to handle logistics at that level, this system will take you one step beyond that! Let's just bypass having to get her to a different location altogether, by selecting LOGISTIC FRIENDLY LOCATIONS.

Same Night Sex System

Most assume that CLUBS are the place to meet women, because they are already in a party mode, but to speed up the process, how about meeting women in places where rooms are available on site, LOL? Or at least pick venues that are adjacent to hotels or your place, or even relocate next to clubs and places where you can easily meet women everyday.

Examples of locations that best support Same Night Sex: Larger trendy hotels, that also include a club, have crowded pool areas, lounges, and restaurants. Places like casinos, resorts and even youth hostels. You either stay there yourself, or focus on women who already have rooms there. The more crowded it is, the higher the odds. Start hanging out in such locations. If concerned about being able to afford being in such places, you do not need to spend much or any money there, when you act like you're at home and smoothly socialize. Even if you live in a small city, go for the closest thing to that, or regularly visit the nearest bigger city.

Next: Sexual subcultures events! Things like tantric sex gatherings, erotic conventions, sex parties and so on. Even regular conventions, seminars, retreats, vacations or social circle functions with pre-established sleeping arrangements. You don't even need to attend the event yourself, just hang out at the hotel where it takes place. I personally Google major hotels conference schedules to find out when such events as hair styling or modeling conferences take place.

In these better locations; focus on situations that are more conducive to sex. For example, women vacationing, partying, or traveling, are more likely to be more permissive and promiscuous. Use that to your own advantage.

S = Selection: Spot the Slut, Logistic Friendly Location and Situations that Are Conducive to Sex!

Finally, the long-term solution is to create a lifestyle that will best support same night sex. For many years I lived at the Hollywood Studio club. A packed apartment complex where mainly singles lived, with great amenities and an insane amount of "in house" parties pretty much every night. Today my wife and I live in a hotel and mini resort by the beach, where on any given day, you stumble on women visiting from all around the world!

> **SNS Gold Nugget:** Find your own "niche" locations that are logistic friendly.

> **Exercise 1: Find Logistic Friendly Location!**
>
> In your own ways, to increase the odds, find your own best logistic friendly location. I gave you a few examples, I know it's a bit of a stretch, but do take that first step! Write down two examples of better locations, or the closest to that, and then mark your calendar and go there within 3 days max!

Your two choices of locations:

_____

_____.

When you are going to go there. Specific DAY and TIME:

_____

_____.

Same Night Sex System

Once you are there, the second step of the selection process will be:

SPOT THE SLUT!!! Women reading, forgive me for the clever play of words, we do want classy women! What I am suggesting is that there's women out there that are more sexually open, ready, and actively seeking, why not focus on them?

To identify them use a question to direct your own focus. Have you ever noticed how we notice more what we pay attention to??? For example, if I start to talk about temperature, you become more aware of whatever the temperature is where you are at, don't you? Same thing with those sexually active women, you'll start to spot and stumble on them, much more when you direct your focus towards recognizing them. The question I personally use as a mantra that I repeat in my mind is "What women here are most sexually open, ready and adventurous?"

SNS Gold Nugget: Focus on women that are more sexually ready!

S = Selection: Spot the Slut, Logistic Friendly Location and Situations that Are Conducive to Sex!

Exercise 2: Question to Spot More Sexual Women!

Write down your own customized question you'll focus on to rapidly spot more sexual women, until it will happen intuitively, and it will. Then start practicing, wherever you go, even if there are only two women there, even if you're not attracted to them. For the fun of it, see if you can identify which one would be more promiscuous. Make sure to only gently focus on the question, trusting your internal guidance. Do it in a non-needy way. We don't want anyone pacing around and looking all creepy because they are overdoing it.

Example: "Which women here are most sexually open, ready and adventurous?"

Create your own example:
_____
_____
_____.

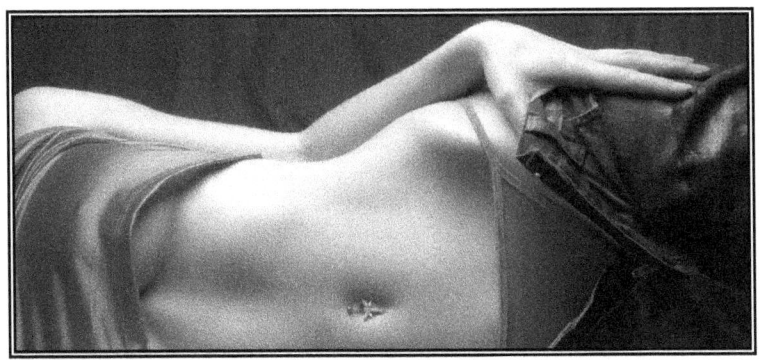

A = Anticipate, Assume, Adventure Frame!

Check your pockets and answer this question: "How many condoms do you have on you right now?" LOL! If you don't have any, you're not anticipating, assuming the part, nor ready for an adventure! Pull out your phone now..." How many numbers of taxi drivers, just in case you needed to rapidly relocate with a girl, do you have in it???" IT'S A BIT BOY SCOUT, BUT BE PREPARED!

1st A: Anticipate what could happen ahead of time!
Women love it when "it just happens," but lots of things can come in the way meanwhile. So to keep it flowing, be aware of, and pre-handle what could be an issue. From being certain you have plenty conveniently, yet discreetly placed condoms, all the way to anticipating who may try to pull her away.

By the way, ALWAYS USE CONDOMS! Make no exceptions, because all it takes is one wrong exception! Even if not that dramatic, things like genital herpes are today so widespread; last I heard the odds where 4 out of 10. Not to mention Aids or pregnancy. **SAFE SEX, OR NO SEX!**

> **Exercise 3: Anticipate by Identifying Best Make-Out and Sex Spot!**
>
> Make it a habit, wherever you are at, to take a moment to anticipate and identify: The best "make-out" and sex spot! Look for more isolated areas that would be sufficiently pleasant for her to want to follow you there. And then think of simple reasons to get her to relocate, for example: "You've got to check out the view on the roof." Do it until it's second nature! COMMIT TO DO THIS EXERCISE!

Either think back to where you went earlier today, or forward to where you're going later. Then wherever it was or maybe, in such location, where would you first relocate for make-out, then for sex? Then write down what you could say to suggest relocating.

> **Example:** "You haven't seen the patio yet? Come on, you MUST check it out!"

Create your own example:
_____
_____
_____

A = Anticipate, Assume, Adventure Frame!

Next part of A is: Assume the part! Men who have spontaneous sex with strangers do so because they expect it. They don't NEED it, but it's part of their reality; they know that sexy women desire them. So right now, how would you carry yourself and walk around if you knew for sure you could easily have sex with hot women TONIGHT??? If you already had sex with several gorgeous girls this week??? If one was blowing you right now, and another one was waiting in your bed??? How would you think of yourself??? If this was so common for you that it'd be no big deal, how much stronger and even greater would that sense of positive sexual expectations now be??? Get the idea???

One of the most potent way to start to more fully assume the part and EXPECT that SEXY WOMEN DO WANT TO SLEEP WITH YOU, is to use guided visualizations and mental rehearsal recordings. If you have the entire SNS Home Study Course, then be certain to listen to your mind programming CDs DAILY!

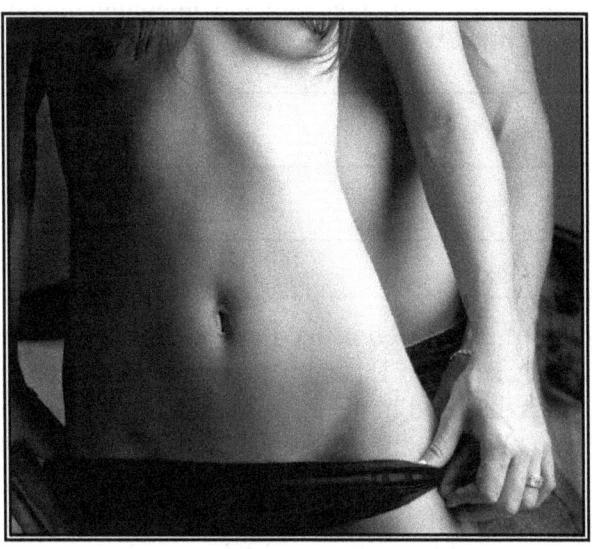

Same Night Sex System

> **Exercise 4: Assume Being Sexually Desired!**
>
> **As you read,** repeat out loud several times...**"Sexy Women Want To Sleep With Me!!!"** Come on; say it again, like you really mean it...Good, again, this time very calmly, with core certainty. Now, just feel and sense it, without even having to say it.... Excellent, now write down your own version! As proper or naughty as you want, from "Delightfully desirable women love to fornicate with me" to "THE HOTTER THEY ARE, THE HARDER THEY WANT ME TO FUCK THEM!!!" Go ahead, write it down and let it echo into your mind a 1000 times. Let it warmly shine and glow into your heart, and powerfully pulse into your royal cock!

Example: "Gorgeous women crave my cock!"

Create your own example:
_____
_____
_____ .

Final part of A is: Adventure Frame! At the live SAME NIGHT SEX seminar, I usually start by holding in one hand, a porn magazine, and in the other hand a romance novel. Then I ask, "What is the difference between them?" On one side a picture of a woman taking it deep and hard, on the other side, well crafted words poetically describing the same thing... "As he held her firmly with his manly hands, she

A = Anticipate, Assume, Adventure Frame!

couldn't believe how big his throbbing cock felt on the inside..." The only difference between what men and women use to fantasize and get off with is that on the ladies' side, THERE'S A PLOT, A STORY, LOL!

Men want to get laid as an accomplishment, and they'll do pretty much anything for it to happen! But what gets women to be more promiscuous and give themselves the permission is the thrill of an erotic adventure. The secret??? DON'T GO OUT TO GET LAID, it's too "average guy," but go out to have and share "adventures!" It's what separates the real men from the little boys, as it will turn you into the real deal versus being just the "pickup" weekend warrior.

SNS Gold Nugget: Average guys live life hoping to get laid, real men live life in a way that makes women want to sleep with them!

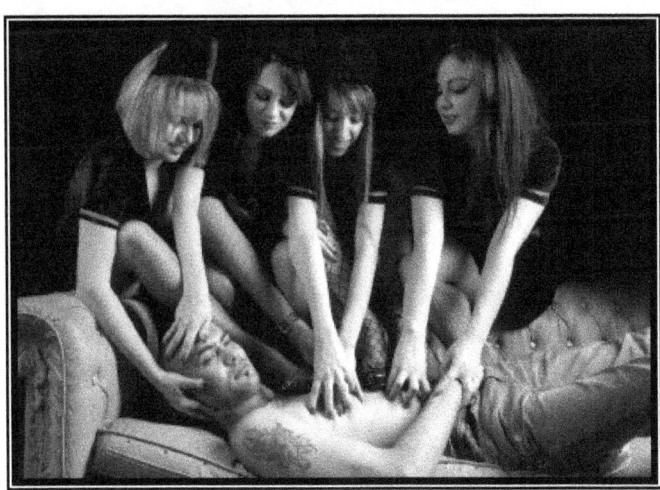

Exercise 5: Have a "Play-date" with Yourself in which Every Step is an Adventure!

Schedule a time for you to go out in the best company that could ever be, YOURSELF! Intelligently turn it into a mischievous, daring, and slightly dangerous adventure. Imagine you are a character in a romance novel, the sexual hero, "How do you carry yourself around and how do you interact with the world, with women???" Go out with that mindset and attitude! I know that for some it may seem silly, but if you wont venture outside of the box, how can you expect that women will? Come on, BE spontaneous, you can do it! Even if only for an hour, TAKE YOURSELF OUT, and be the most fun, spontaneous, exciting, fascinating company you can be to yourself during that time, up to a point where other people would want part of it.

BONUS EXERCISE, at no extra charge!!!

First chance to go out and buy at least 50 condoms, DO IT! DO IT! DO IT! If you already have condoms, BUY MORE!

M = Middle Ground - Finding Your SEXUAL EQUILIBRIUM!

Once you have your condoms, it may create a bit of unhealthy pressure, and we do not want that. Our next step is to find a balance, "THE MIDDLE GROUND", where most men tend to go extreme against their own benefits.

On one side, it is easy for us men to become obsessed with "getting laid." Go to any club in the world, and watch how ridiculously overly zealous and needy most guys are! No wonder women tend to avoid dudes like that! On the other side, we've all at times, been so passive and wimpy about it, we never got it! So the secret is to develop your ability to simultaneously set a true resolution that YOU ARE GOING TO HAVE SEX NOW...while staying ZEN about it, being above it, and allowing it the time needed.

I remember the first "same night sex" I had after a dry period of 4 years following the dramatic ending of my first marriage! I was staying with a few buddies in Del Mar CA, by the racetrack, and was so fed up with it, I told them, "I am going to go out now and get laid, DO NOT LET ME BACK

Same Night Sex System

HERE UNTIL I GET LAID, and IF I DON'T BY MONDAY (it was Saturday), I owe you each $300!" Much more than I could afford to waste at the time.

It actually took 24 hours, and I did get laid!

When you combine such extreme level of resolution with a more complete surrender to just have fun and experiment, it will provide you with the magic vibe that is the ultimate turn on for women: "He wants me bad, but he doesn't need to have me!" "He could take me now, but he could also leave and never regret it!"

SNS Gold Nugget: Most men are either too sexually passive or aggressive! Be committed, but unattached, such combined power and poise will drive women wild!

Exercise 6, part 1: Find "The Middle Ground"!

Create your own list of combined opposites, to find that middle ground, and correct past tendencies to lean toward either side too much.

Examples: BE FORWARD, BUT NOT FORCEFUL - BE SEXUAL, BUT NOT SLEEZY - BE POWERFULLY DRIVEN, BUT NOT NEEDY - BE COMMITTED, BUT NOT DEPENDENT!

M = Middle Ground - Finding Your SEXUAL EQUILIBRIUM!

Create your own examples:
_____

_____

_____.

> **Exercise 6, Part 2: Embody the Ideal Sexual Vibe Energy!**
>
> Go walk around any crowded place, and using your breathing, focus, body, and above phrases, access that natural more balanced place between having a strong sexual intention, and just appreciating women without any agenda! Observe yourself leaning too much to one side or the other, until you find your own **SEXUAL EQUILIBRIUM**. It may take some time.

A very potent advanced way, as a demonstration to yourself, the Universe, and WOMEN, that you are mastering this balance, is to choose NOT to masturbate at all for at least 21 days. SEX AS A CHOICE, INSTEAD OF A NEED OR ADDICTION. You may get so tired of not climaxing, that it becomes your leverage to GET A CHICK TONIGHT!!! It will work wonders for your self-esteem, and the subtle ways in which women perceive you. It took me a long time to achieve this, and I call it "The Seduction Final Frontier", but when I did, I started to notice women noticing me in a whole new way. As if they can sense that I love sex but don't need it! Not for everybody, but if you are daring and curious, try it! Unless I was wrong in my perception that most men jerk off, and I just confessed I used to do it, Oh My God, LOL...

E - Evoke Her Sexual Side!

There are 4 main responses we can bring out of women, and all women are capable of all 4, and will at different times respond to different guys in different ways.

- Lowest one is **AVOIDANCE:** From a milder polite excuse to straight up repulsion.
- Next one up is **FRIENDSHIP:** From casual acquaintance to being her girl friend with a penis.

By the way, it's OK to have female friends. You do want lots of female friends, but you don't want to evoke friendship in the ones you want beyond that.

- Second to top is **RELATIONSHIP:** From casual dating to more long-term commitments.
- Top one is **SEXUALITY:** From one night stands to fuck buddies.

So the trick is to evoke the one that will best support your intention! Since we're talking about same night sex, BE VERY CAUTIOUS to only steer in the sexual direction. In general, women tend to not sleep right away with a guy they see as possible "relationship material," because they don't want him to want that with other women after, and women who sleep with a guy right away, tend to not want a possible relationship with him after, out of fear he may just sleep with other girls.

Here's then what to avoid when what you want is just to share a SEXY EXPERIENCE:

Any question or topic that evokes a DATING AND RELATIONSHIP FRAME.

> **Examples:** "So what are you're looking for in a man?" Or "What is most important to you in a relationship?" Or "Are you seeing someone right now?" Screw that! It's completely irrelevant for same night sex! Save such questions for women you are screening for long-term relationships.

By the way, as a side note, keep an open mind and enjoy all of the seasons and flavors of your sex and love life. Leave it to frustrated stuck up chumps to limit themselves to only one type of sexual fulfillment. Life is too rich not to explore all your best options. Many awesome pickup and dating experts, including myself, Adam Lyons, and James Marshal from Australia, and soon Speer (whom just got engaged at the time of this writing), after years of wild experiences, are now super happily married.

So stay open and receptive, and keep in mind that all that you learn for and from same night sex may also one day serve you to drive that one ideal girl so wild in bed, she'll only want you! And as you'll meet greater, hotter, and more and more fascinating women, you do not have to run away after you fuck them, out of fear of commitment. Whatever you choose let it be out of more possibilities, not less!

Meanwhile, to evoke sexuality, focus on everything that supports SEX NOW! How about bringing out her sense of playfulness, outrageousness, mischievousness, and her wilder side! To do that, you can use questions, topics, and most of all, role-playing, games, and activities that have these pre-sex components.

My personal preferred conversation theme to lead to sex...
"When something is sooo good, you want it sooo bad, you have to have it right now…"

Be certain to also fully assume and embrace your desires as a man, and not apologize for them. You'd be amazed at how direct you can be and sexually forward from the start when it comes from the balanced placed we talked about. Mentally rehearse being more sexually aggressive!

SNS Gold Nugget: No matter who the woman is, there's always a guy or type of men that will bring out her sexuality, BE THAT PERSON!

Exercise 7, Part 1: What Have You Been Invoking?

Reflect on recent interactions with women. What part of them did you bring out? Avoidance? Friendship? Relationship? Or sexuality?

Exercise 7, Part 2: What Part Do You Want to Bring Out?
Make a list of the sub-sexual ingredients you want to evoke such as DARINGNESS, EAGERNESS, URGENCY, PLAYFULNESS, ETC.

Same Night Sex System

Create your own list of sub-sexual elements:

_____

_____

_____

_____

_____

_____.

N = Negation - Matching and Leading
The Natural Female Permission Model!

Negation serves to more powerfully and pleasantly lead women in the way that best works for them. With recreational sex, women are facing a dilemma in which they are torn between doing what is proper and their desire, GOOD GIRL, BAD GIRL! To best assist them through this opposite pull, negation will allow you to help honor the initial tendency to hold back, and come up with excuses to not look like a slut, while still moving forward and getting more and more sexual.

The basic concept behind negation is that at the level of thoughts, we cannot process a negative without at least thinking about it. For example, if I say, "Whatever you do, do not become aware of your breathing..." even if you don't want to comply, you'll still become aware of it, at least briefly. When you use this with women, it doesn't mean they will act on it, but it will certainly at least arouse their imagination.

The two main types of negation are:

1. Proactive Negation: To be used ahead of time. Whenever you sense hesitation on her side to take the next step, state it before she does. Example, as soon as you notice the first few signs of holding back on her part, tell her, "We probably shouldn't go all the way now." To make sure it doesn't reinforce the wrong direction, state it towards what "Not to do" and add to it a touch of acknowledging how pleasant it really is or could be as well... "But it feels so good." And of course, even though you're saying, "Let's not", you continue. ISN'T THAT EXACTLY WHAT WOMEN TEND TO DO? Don't they often say what they are not going to do at first, then end up doing it? In all my sexual adventures, at one point or another, even the nastiest and wildest girls did momentarily express that they shouldn't!

2. Recovery Negation: To be used to redirect after she gets hung up, to reassure her and move on. Example, if she says... "We really shouldn't, not now, not here." Answer "Of course we shouldn't," AGREEMENT to re-hook her, followed by NEGATION, "It's not like we're going to HAVE THE WILDEST SEX EVER, RIGHT HERE AND RIGHT NOW, and you'll so WANT ME, you won't even care". In the second part, you tell her what to do and can get overly graphic since you're only saying you're not going to DO IT.

Beyond the fun tool of negation, the goal is to process her negation in a new light, not as a red light, but your first green light. However you deal with it, be ready, as it is one of the biggest LANDMARKS that will make or break same night sex. Even with the most sexually forward chicks, it's part of being a woman. They are not saying no, just asking for help in not having to feel shameful.

*N = Negation: Matching and Leading
The Natural Female Permission Model!*

It's wise to add to this, especially if you are new, that there may also be times when a woman is just plainly saying no. And that's OK; she's free to do that! Learn how to recognize the difference! And remember, we powerful men, who can have plenty women, never have to force a woman beyond what she's comfortable doing at the time, or ever.

To clarify, techniques like negation are not meant to TRICK women into bed, but to support them all the way through the process as only a superior man with a greater understanding of what women need, would.

SNS Gold Nugget: A woman's way to allow herself to say YES, often starts with a temporary NO to honor her need not to feel too much like a slut.

Exercise 8, Part 1:
Don't be Fooled by What Comes First!

List things you've heard women say to slow down the process, and practice leading the negation while emphasizing DOING IT, and reminding her how pleasant it is. Example: "We really shouldn't GO FOR IT ALL THE WAY...But it feels so good!"

What she said: _____.

Create an example of negation to handle it:
_____
_____.

Same Night Sex System

What she said: _____.

Create an example of negation to handle it:

_____

_____.

What she said: _____.

Create an example of negation to handle it:

_____

_____.

Exercise 8, Part 2: Stay Grounded Regardless!

Decide right now that from now on, you'll stay very calm in a sexy and grounded way when women first say NO as their way to start saying YES!

I = Information Gathering - The "5 Ps" Elicitation Questions!

To better preemptively handle whatever logistical issue could come in the way of great sexual experiences, there are a few standard things you must know about the women you meet as soon as possible.

NOW, FIRST GROUND RULE OF SAME NIGHT SEX INFORMATION GATHERING IS: Focus primarily on what is relevant for sex to happen RIGHT THERE, RIGHT THEN!

For that, what you need to know is:

Purpose: Why she's there.
People: Whom she's there with, and what's their relationship.
Place: Where she's staying THAT NIGHT! Not where she lives (unless they're one and the same).
Plan: What she's doing later on THAT NIGHT and next morning.
Person who is driving: Her or somebody else.

These are simple questions, but often guys will ask them in ways that are too telegraphed, average and boring.

Example of what to avoid: "So how did you get here tonight? Oh really, and where are you staying? Oh great, and who's here with you?" (Snoring)! Come on, what's next??? What's your sign and what do you do for a living? LOL! Such "interview like" successions of typical questions only steer women toward AVOIDANCE, or friendship and dating at best! And even if they politely answer, that doesn't mean they are getting closer to wanting SEX NOW!

Keep in mind that the main reason women use to justify sleeping with a guy is: **"He's not like every other guy"**, so a short cut to natural attraction and arousal is to simply BE THE GUY WHO'S NOT LIKE EVERY OTHER GUY!!! Because THAT'S THE GUY who gets laid! And THAT GUY from now on IS YOU!

So make sure that you...

1. Avoid successions of questions! Go for one question, then play with her some, to keep on building sexual tension, until you get back to the next question, and so on, ALTERNATE!

2. Make sure your questions are fun! Avoid typical conversational questions; turn your questions into quizzes, challenges, cold reads and games! BUT DO KEEP IT SIMPLE, direct and authentic!

3. Ask them more dominantly and playfully! Beyond what we say, it's how we say it that matters most! Even though you are asking, continue to lead! Women only give poor answers to guys who ask poorly!

And here's a little secret: Often people will reveal more about themselves to correct a false statement, than when asked questions!

I = Information Gathering - The "5 Ps" Elicitation Questions!

So one advanced option I personally use a lot is: I presuppose things in my questions that I don't know yet. This way, if I am off, in correcting me, she'll tell me all I needed to know, or my guess will have been confirmed.

If let's say she's holding an alcoholic beverage, tell her... "What kind of a designated driver are you??? Look at you sipping that drink..." Or to find out if she has a boyfriend there, "Hey, if you're going to flirt with me, let's not do it right in front of your boyfriend; he's looking at us."

And remember the golden rule of communication:
DO WHAT WORKS! Focus only on what causes her to respond! Don't let the conversation depend on the approach, make the approach depend on the conversation.

Of course, if you play high-end hotels game as I suggested in step one, or any locations where women may have rooms to stay, all you really need is ONE QUESTION: "How are you and your boyfriend enjoying the rooms here?" This way you'll know what is most important right away: Is she staying there indeed? And is she without a man? Or is she with one but doesn't seem to care?

SNS Gold Nugget: If you only ask questions, it can soon sound like an interview, and lose its sex appeal. So balance questions and play to build sexual tension, while you get all the information you need to see if she's a good candidate for SAME NIGHT SEX.

Exercise 9: Write one "ABOVE AVERAGE" question for each of the 5 main things you must find out:

35

Same Night Sex System

Purpose: Why she's there. Write down your example:
_____
_____
_____.

People: Whom she's there with, and what's their relationship. Write down your example:
_____
_____
_____.

Place: Where she's staying THAT NIGHT! Not where she lives (unless they're one and the same). Write down your example:
_____
_____
_____.

Plan: What she's doing later on THAT NIGHT and next morning. Write down your example:
_____
_____
_____.

I = Information Gathering - The "5 Ps" Elicitation Questions!

Person who is driving: How she got there. Write down your example:

_____

_____

_____.

Once you wrote one example for each question, practice asking them in playful and dominant ways. Experiment until you get women to eagerly answer these questions, while their sexual interest continues to grow!

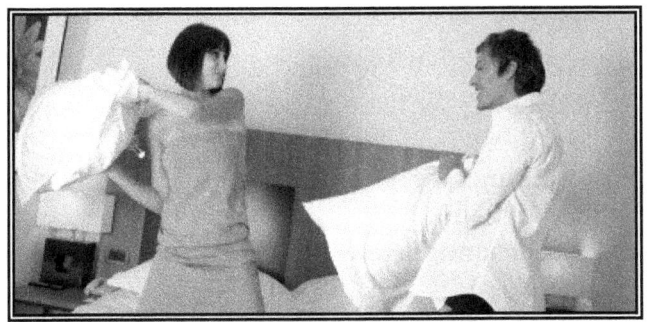

G = Games and Role Play for SEXUAL CONDUCTIVITY!

Both in real life adventures or romantic comedies, when you pay attention to what takes place just before sex, you'll notice that it's usually some form of fun physical interaction: Playful wrestling, dancing, pillow fighting, or accidentally being stuck in the rain and having to run together to find cover! As cliché as these examples may sound, we want to do what happens naturally that leads to sex, rather than relying on conversation, which by itself, is much less conducive to sex.

A fast way to get her going and bring sexual elements as early as possible is to introduce games and role-play, since they are done in a seemingly innocent manner!

The goal is to rapidly create a dynamic in which you'll find elements of...

- **Sexuality:** Sexual Themes.
- **Proximity and touch:** We're having a private experience.
- **Frolicking:** We're having fun in a frisky light-spirited manner.
- **Serendipity:** It feels like this is meant to be.
- **Secrecy:** We're the only ones who know this.

Same Night Sex System

- **Adventure:** We're doing something exciting.
- **Mischief:** We're doing something we probably shouldn't do, but who cares.
- **Bonding:** We're on the same page, getting closer and closer.
- **Exclusion:** There's us, and then there's the rest of the world.

Because usually, wherever you find these elements, you also find PEOPLE HAVING SEX LATER!!! I call this **SEXUAL CONDUCTIVITY!**

Here's an example as a reference for you to play with, until you're able to naturally come up with your own games on the spot! Pay attention to the presence of the elements I just listed above.

As you position yourself side to side, tell her: "OK, look around and let's play **'Who's had some, who's had none!'** ready?"

Because you're going to talk about other people, in order to not be heard, it makes it OK to position yourself closer to her. It also causes the "You and her versus the rest" dynamic, plus the topic is now of a sexual nature.

Then pinpoint the most unlikely person to have had sex and say "Over there, for sure, so recent, probably didn't even get to wash."

After goofing around about it for a bit, look at her and say, "What about you, let me see...?" Whether you first playfully guess or she answers before you do, use whatever comes up to have fun together.

G = Games and Role Play for SEXUAL CONDUCTIVITY!

When role-playing, to avoid being too "Heavy" and "Transparent" and to better build sexual tension, I like to use what I call "DUAL DIRECTION GAME ™".

For example, as a reply to her answering one of my more sexual questions, I'll jokingly tell her, "You pervert," but at the same time tickle and wrestle her in rather permissively forward manner. So my words seem to be moving away from being sexual, while my body's going in full force. Or vice-versa. I'll teasingly say, "Mmm...wait until I take care of you tonight, no sex you had before will even count or compare..." and lean my body back like I am about to leave. And to reinforce that "Pull/Push" even more, every 3 to 4 times you synchronize and go in strong and direct, both with your words and body. In the end, sex is very much like dancing. Lead her without stepping on her toes, don't go too fast or too slow, then powerfully pick her up once in a while.

Silly ideas for role-play: Act out a confession, and then spank her sins out! Do a pretend wedding on the spot, then grab her and walk away for honeymoon sex! Act out ways that people would use to approach each other in the past. Start with first politely and very properly courting her, as in the Renaissance, then just grabs her and go cave man on her, as in prehistoric days.

Make sure that you get her to be proactive, to avoid being the "Queens Fool", there to only amuse and entertain her! She HAS to do her part too. Sex is a give and take experience. Induce reciprocity from the start, meaning SHE HAS TO PITCH IN and OFFER YOU VALUE TOO!

One way to do that, is you initiate then tell her, "OK, your turn now." Regularly reverse the roles.

Same Night Sex System

Be certain to ground these playful, wild episodes into moments of deeper connection, like two lovers who just had sex! So you also appeal to her need for comfort by being more than just the "funny guy", but the truly multi-dimensional romantic hero she'll sexually surrender to. And by momentarily shifting gears, it tends to cause her to then go further on the next round!

> **SNS Gold Nugget:** The deeper benefit of games and role-playing is that it also helps fulfill women's need to justify ACTING MORE SEXUALLY.

Exercise 10: Create Your Own Fun Sexy Games!

Rather than giving you an actual routine, to help you start to create your own games on the spot, I will simply give you a topic that you'll turn into a game leading to role-play. Be certain it includes the pre-sex elements we mentioned: **Sexuality, proximity and touch, frolicking, serendipity, secrecy, adventure, mischief, bonding, and exclusion.** The topic is "Whom here is most likely to have sex tonight". At least come up with basic idea! Have fun!

Create your own example of a game and some role-playing: _____

_____

_____.

H = Hierarchy - How to Find The One Step She'll Take Regardless!

The average guy will try to unbutton, unzip, pull her pants down and take her panties off, ALL IN ONE SHOT, and on top of that, probably before she even wants him to do that. The Same Night Sex Expert will get HER to do it all at once HERSELF, because once a woman really wants you, you'll be the one having to slow her down.

I once seduced this girl so efficiently, she started to blow me while I was driving and FORTUNATELY traffic was slow, because I lightly hit the car in front. Not to mention the fact that people could see us in cars around. Not only did I SELECT the type of girl who would do that, it was the accumulation of all the steps I took before that lead her there.

So Hierarchy is the art of building her desire, one step at a time, like you would slowly start a campfire, until she craves it so bad, she'll do the work. If you've ever started a campfire, you know the secret is "Never more or less than needed", so you neither suffocate nor deprive the first few sparks. Then keep on fueling. So creating a hierarchy is like putting together an array of options. While most guys either get loads of resistance because they try to go from A to Z in just one shot, or get zero compliance because they never get started, us we're going to intelligently built it one step at a time AS FAST AS POSSIBLE, finding just the right rhythm that she can only surrender to.

You'll do so at the following 3 levels:

1. General compliance: Getting her to go along with what is being offered and suggested.

2. Location compliance: Leading her closer to a place where you can have sex.

3. Sexual compliance: Getting her to act on her arousal.

To clarify, these steps are taken to benefit both you and her, by creating a smoother experience, not in a manipulative manner.

SNS Gold Nugget: A woman may not go all the way, right away, BUT, even if minimal at first, there's always a step she CAN and WILL take right now, that leads her closer to sex with you. Find out what that step is!

Exercise 11: Trace It Back from The Bedroom!

H = Hierarchy - How to Find the One Step She'll Take Regardless!

Let's establish a trajectory starting first with the end result, all the way to the first step you take towards it. Write down the hierarchy of steps to connect the dots between hello and sex, as a way to help you better pace and lead the women you'll meet. The purpose is to help you begin to look at the bigger picture and create roadmaps as references. To end up somewhere, it helps to know where we're going and how to get there.

Start with the end first, and trace it back all the way, one step at a time, to train your mind to naturally do so when face to face.

Example: We are having sex on the roof of the hotel. We got there to see the view. I brought up the topic of "What one daring thing we could do to make this night more memorable". We relocated there by role-playing that we were spies. I kept on getting physical by pretending someone was coming and we had to take cover, so I would protect her by putting my body in front of her. Before that, at the bar, the topic of being spies came up when I asked her what would be her choice of most dangerously exhilarating lifestyle, out of the 3 following options: **Spy, Bank Robber, or Pimp.** When she picked spy, I playfully pretended that I was holding her at gunpoint, saying, "Whom do you work for? Who sent you?" I then told her we had been spotted and had to fly away with the helicopter that awaited us on the roof. Then grounded it by saying..."Seriously the view is incredible up there, come on 007, you have to see it, before they get to us, we only live once..." etc. Get the idea?

Same Night Sex System

Write down your own imaginary scenario from sex all the way back to hello. Think of ideas to "connect the dots" and transition smoothly.

_____
_____
_____
_____
_____
_____
_____
_____
_____
_____.

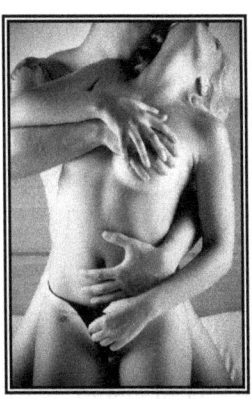

T = Time Focus - Triggering The "Fuck it, I Want This Now" Mind Set!

Since sex is so pleasant, why don't more people just do it on the spot with strangers??? Two main reasons: Consequences and Moral Issues! And these are even greater for women, who face things like pregnancy and the reputation of being a slut. BUT, it's also true that we all, at times, act more impulsively and indulge, for example when women shop or go for sweets.

Often what causes us to go for urges rather than reason depends on WHAT POINT IN TIME WE FOCUS ON. For example, if a woman is out but focused on the fact she has to get up the next day to work, looking at it from that perspective, she may not find it appropriate to have sex with someone she just met. But if focused on how the opportunity may never show again in the future, LONG-TERM focus, it may create a sense of urgency that will overrule her concerns. That explains how some have sex one last time before getting married!

The other position in time that tends to omit consequences or moral issues is EXTREME SHORT-TERM focus, thinking only about right now! Most behaviors that people embrace when partying come from that place when you think about it. This is also what causes people to sustain addictions, despite danger of consequences.

So whether INDULGENCE comes from the URGENCY caused by fear of missing out in the LONG RUN, or the omission of possible consequences due to focusing strictly on SHORT-TERM pleasure, the ability to emphasize "GOING FOR IT NOW" may come handy to expedite the process.

Often time, it's MID-TERM focus that gets in the way! Her thinking about her other plans that week, or what her friends may say later, etc. But IMMEDIATE FOCUS, or SUPER LONG-TERM FOCUS are more likely to get her to just say "FUCK IT...I want this now...Why not..." and indulge.

Using time focus, I personally even caused girls to choose to miss flights to be able to sleep with me one more time. A bit selfish at the time, I admit it, nevertheless, truly potent.

Here's an example of a question you can use for that:

"If you were 80 years old now and you could come back through time for JUST ONE NIGHT, and re-experience the freshness of your young hot body ONE LAST TIME, but you could only do one thing with it...Which of the following 3 options would you pick?"

a. "Get a tattoo on your tight butt before it gets wrinkly, once again."

*T = Time Focus –
Triggering The "Fuck it, I Want This Now" Mind Set!*

---

b. "A passionate night of the most incredible sex you ever had, so strong, you'll still be thinking about it when being 80."

c. "Help an old lady shower and dress because you would know how it's not easy."

Then of course, whatever choice she makes, tease her about it, don't be the average guy who gets horny when she picks the sex, and disappointed if she doesn't. Plus it's irrelevant; the goal is not for her to openly pick the sex answer, but to cause her to put things in the perspective of time, to create URGENCY!

SNS Gold Nugget: There's two points of focus in time that tend to get us to say, "Fuck it, let's DO IT NOW:" Immersion in the pleasure of the moment, or the long-term possibility of never having it again. Use both to encourage ACTING ON THIS NOW!

**Exercise 12, Part 1:
"I GOTTA HAVE THIS NOW!"**

Come up with one personal or general true story that emphasizes a "Fuck it, I want this now!" attitude, and bring up that topic in your interactions with women. Then find out what causes such responses for them??? Chocolate? Shopping? Ice cream? Then escalate the conversation towards topics like "When we so crave something we HAVE TO HAVE IT NOW!"

Write your example:

_____

_____

_____

Exercise 12, Part 2:
Immersion in the Immediate Moment!

By being totally present with them, physically, mentally and emotionally in how pleasant the moment is, help women you interact with to do the same. Pay attention to how YOUR presence enhances THEIR presence, and purposely IMMERSE yourself into the experience. IN A NON-NEEDY WAY! Because you are having a good time, not because it could "pay off"!

S = Sexual Frames - Reasons to Justify Sexual Actions!

Women want sex as much or even more than we do, but social condoning doesn't always make it easy for them to give themselves the permission. So part of being a powerful sexual suitor is to assist them to feel free to act on their desires without guilt or remorse. Providing superior ways to look at having sex with you that will take women above moral inner struggles best does this.

First, how are you looking at it on your side? Are you hopping to "screw some chick" just so you can get relief and boost your ego? Or are you aiming to have the hottest and most fun sexual adventure for both? Are your own frames pre-determined to make women feel immoral and shameful, or are they geared toward giving women more options to be sexually fulfilled and liberated?

Then, you will help women frame their own experience in a way that will make it easier to FREELY ENJOY! The goal is to set sexual frames that will help women justify their actions, and eliminate their concerns!

Examples of typical concerns women tend to have that could hold them back:

- **The opinion of other people:** Fear of being judged by peers.
- **Buyer's remorse:** Fear of regretting their decision.
- **Feeling like a slut:** Fear of being too easy.

Examples of typical reasons women use to justify their actions:

- **Greatness:** This guy is so awesome; I better not miss this opportunity!
- **Serendipity:** It's meant to be, it's beyond my control!
- **Deservingness:** I have the right to have this now!

It's also important to encourage her to make the decision based on her needs, and not other people's need. What we call frames of SELF-REFERENCE!

The formula to create frames is simple:

Link what women most want to "doing it," and what they least want to "not doing it." And by the way, isn't every possible ways to look at sex the result of an association? Putting two things in the same box? Example: "A woman having sex with a stranger is a slut!" Says whom? So you'll simply start to reverse these judgments!

And to save you some time, here's THE MOTHER OF ALL SEXUAL FRAMES you want to emphasize: **It takes**

S = Sexual Frames - Reasons to Justify Sexual Actions!

a superior woman to GO FOR IT! I personally will frame the ability to feel free to act sexually as a sign that she is more fully in touch with her own femininity.

I'll even ask women directly: **"How well in tune with your own sexuality would you say you are?"** Then in my explanation why I am asking, I will list all of what could be in the way as being a sign of lack of being in tune with it, and all that will serve as a sign of being in tune with it.

> **Example:** "I am asking because so many women are so out of touch with their own sexuality, they let society, family or their girlfriends decide for them instead of **listening to your own needs** and what **you really desire**. **Me**, I think that for a woman to more fully blossom into her true sexual fulfillment, she must first set aside all the garbage judgments society makes on powerful independent women, and become the ruler of her own sexuality. Like Cleopatra, she was one of the first women, when you think about it, that's responsible for all the progress the sexual revolution brought in freeing women and encouraging equality.

Notice how I even link "doing it" to feminism, women's freedom and rights, etc. I even had straight up lesbians go for it with me after framing it properly! I must also tell you that this IS what I believe deep down inside, not just tricks. So your turn now to embrace sexual frames so freeing, women will want to share them with you, to their own benefits. Of course, your frames will be different if focused more on one special girl, then you frame commitment as the pinnacle, to the benefit of the relationships quality and longevity.

SNS Gold Nugget: The sexual frame that most matters is yours! Because when it is truly freeing to women, their own limiting frames won't measure up!

Exercise 13: Sexually Healing Frames!

Write down your own explanation of why "sleeping with you" is the best choice sexy women can make now! Don't just do so in a way that will serve and be flattering to you. Also do it in a way that is super highly appealing to women and would make them feel free to do it with you now!

Sexy women MUST enjoy sex with me right now, because:

_____

_____

_____

_____

_____

_____

_____

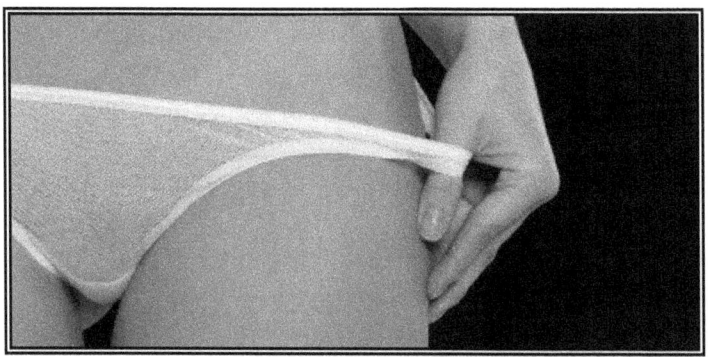

E = Escalating Sexually - Get Passed the Panties!

Ever had women push your hand away when you tried to touch their breast or unbutton their pants? And what about her taking her hand away too soon when you thought she finally was going to go for your cock? Why is that??? It's because men and women are wired differently when it comes to how we process arousal.

Porn stars drive men wild because they know how to get to it right away, just like we like it as men. So be the equivalent of that to women by becoming the sexual suitor from romance novels and giving it to them the way they most want it!

Typical Male Arousal Process: "I want her to grab my dick and suck and ride it fast and hard until I blow my load on her face".

Typical Female Arousal Process: "I want him to drive me wild one little wave of pleasure at a time until I can't take it anymore and I want him to take me".

Male and female arousal processes are like two different roads, driving to the same place. And you'll get there faster when using HER "PLEASURE MAP" to get her there.

Most guys have it backwards, they do too much too soon, causing her to slow down, and then fail to take leadership and dominantly give her pleasure when she's ready! So here's the secret escalation recipe to drive women wild up to the point where they'll want you so bad, all their rules and reasons to resist will no longer exist.

You will apply this model to any step forward toward sex, from the very first touch when you meet her, through the pre-sex foreplay as you're relocating, all the way to being inside of her, whatever the sex location will be.

Get Past the Panties!

Step 1. Get to the edge and stay there for a bit. By edge, I mean the furthest she can comfortably take it at the time.

Example: Moving sideways, lightly caress the stitching of the top of her underwear.

Step 2. Take it away, almost right away. You do that to make sure you condition wanting more, not resistance.

Example: Take it in the opposite direction by slowly sliding your fingers up her spine.

Step 3. Go to neutral pleasant place. This will help to sufficiently sustain the arousal, while causing her to be the one who wants your hand back toward her underwear.

E = Escalating Sexually - Get Passed the Panties!

Example: Massage and her neck, making little circles, and squeeze lightly here and there.

Step 4. Take her by surprise by going for the unexpected. Do it passionately, mixing dominance and comfort.

Example: Lift her up against the wall and pull her body toward you while you press yourself against her. Then reach for her panties from underneath now, and if experienced enough, rip them off.

Lead the back and forth dance of escalation the right way, and you'll built so much sexual tension, she'll end up ripping your clothes off.

SNS Gold Nugget: The more you gradually escalate on your side, the more directly she will on her side. So both of you get it the way you want it! Isn't that what awesome sex is about?

Exercise 14: Be the Sexual Hero of Your Own Romance Novel!

To learn to arouse women the way that will drive them wild, write a 3 page essay on an imaginary passionate night of spontaneous sex with one or more gorgeous girls craving you so badly, they have to have you. NOW HERE'S THE CHALLENGE: Got to be written in a way that would totally arouse even the most conservative girl out there!

Same Night Sex System

Title of your erotic essay:

1.

E = Escalating Sexually - Get Passed the Panties!

2.

Same Night Sex System

_____
_____
_____
_____
_____
_____
_____
_____
_____
_____
_____
_____
_____
_____3.

X = The X-tra Ingredient - How to Tap Into Divine Pussy Providence!

Now here's the ultimate question??? Breathe and take a moment to imagine the hottest kind of woman you most would love to have sex with tonight. See what she looks like; picture this sexy girl in your mind.

Then ask yourself, "What kind of man would this girl most want to have sex with tonight?"

Unless you answered "ME" (you the reader), and assuming that it was what actually popped to mind genuinely, then we have work to do! Because realize that WE GET THE WOMEN WE THINK WE CAN HAVE, not the ones we want! So I know there's probably loads of hot girls you see daily that you would love to have sex with. But the real issue here is "Do you see YOURSELF as the guy THEY would want to sleep with?"

And until the answer is a strong and authentic YES, then you must give correcting this matter all that you have, because the future of your sexual fulfillment depends on it! For those who's sense of sexual value is already equal to or above the perceived sexual value of the women they most desire, then just explore way beyond that! Self-esteem is something you can always have more of!

So that magical X-tra ingredient is YOUR SEXUAL SELF-IMAGE. It's the law of attraction and secret to manifestation, we get what we think we can get, not what we want. Bottom line is guys who get to have same night sex are guys who expect they will. Men who bed top looking women know they can, because it's part of their reality. Sure, they know they can because they have, but it also works the other way around.

That is why those who accidentally "get lucky" and bed a woman they didn't think would want to be with them, tend to mess it up pretty rapidly and lose her, because they viewed it as the exception but not the rule. So you MUST RAISE your sense of sexual value so it matches or surpasses the value you attach to sexy women. Once you do that, any shyness, anxiety, and sexual hesitation will vanish. But it is a process, and one that may take a little time.

To help you speed up the process, if you have the full Same Night Sex home study course, use the programming CDs that come with it. If you only have the book, it is a good start, and allow me to recommend you upgrade and get the CDs too.

However you'll go about it, mind conditioning is extremely potent and we have plenty resources that will help you with that. Another great recommendation is our classic program called "The Feminine Voice of Seduction", a series of guided visualizations and affirmations spoken by women to see yourself as the man hot girls want to have sex with.

SNS Gold Nugget: Raise your sense of sexual deservingness until it matches the value you put on the women you most desire. It also helps to STOP overvaluing their sex-appeal.

Exercise 15: Evening Sexual Self-Image Strengthening!

With the support of conditioning CDs or at least in your mind to start with, preview yourself being truly sexually fulfilled! EVERY NIGHT shower your subconscious with a refreshing new sense of sexual possibilities, power and POTENCY! DO IT EVERY NIGHT!

✳ ✳ ✳

Section Two:

Same Night Sex MECHANICS!

*7 Simple Steps to
Speed Up the Sexual Process!*

Step 1. Sexual Leadership - It's Not Going to Suck Itself!

Let's say you're having a great conversation in a public place with a girl you just met, even if she's totally into you, the odds of her grabbing you by the hand to bring you to her car or the bathroom, and beg you to take her right there and then, are not the highest! Because even when women most desire you, you'll most likely have to be the one to connect the dots and make it happen!

And that's why, even if you naturally attract women easily, you'll need powerful ways to lead and orchestrate the experience!

Now the mechanics you're about to discover are designed specifically for SAME NIGHT SEX, and may not always apply, or differ slightly, or need to be combined with other elements if focusing on other options to meet women, such as day game, social circle game, dating or long-term relationships. We have plenty other resources I can recommend for that. Nevertheless, all you learn here will, overall, make you a much more sexually appealing man.

Step 2. Sexual Screening - How to Sexually Open and Qualify from the Start!

Once you have the mindset and foundation that will support it, when it comes to the mechanics, if you want sex on the same night, best is to go sexual from the start! This will help you to test how sexually forward and ready she is. Keep in mind; if she can't handle much at the beginning of the interaction, she probably won't handle much more later on.

So yes, it is a numbers game, and to save time you find out right away if she sexually qualifies! If she doesn't, move on, another one will. But remember that since you are a source of pleasure for women, you leave the women you have talked to in a way that is so attractive; they wish you had stayed!

Even if they had a poor attitude, keep your sex appeal and vibe clean and high for the ones to come. It's also important to make the difference between SEX APPEAL and SLEAZINESS. Make sure you come across the right way when going in SEXUAL!

Same Night Sex System

Here are 3 options to go in sexual, as a way to TEST THEIR READINESS! To choose which type to go for, pay attention to the situation and current state of the women you approach. For each one, I'll also give you a basic follow up idea.

Option one, STRONG INTENTION! Powerfully and directly communicate that you like, you choose, and you desire her!

> **Example: "It's just that I find you so incredibly SEXY!"** Followed by something like **"OK, you're warned, if you continue to act that way, I am just going to have to talk to you!"** Of course, said playfully. Then talk to her.

Option two, REVERSED INTENTION! Playfully act as if SHE'S the one who desires you!

> **Example: "That's cute how you're acting all sexy just so I will talk to you, OK, I'll play along!"** Then you can ask her **"So how often does that work for you, you just pick on the guy you want and try to seduce him???"** Notice what is presupposed.

Option three, SOFT INTENTION! More vaguely refer to sex!

> **Example: "I sense a rather pleasant sexy vibe from you, have you had sex on your mind lately? You should hide it better, it totally shows!"** You can then continue with a question such as **"Do you believe it's possible to tell who is thinking about sex, and who is not, look around, can you tell???"**

Step 2. Sexual Screening -
How to Sexually Open and Qualify from the Start!

> **Exercise: How to Sexually Open and Qualify from the Start!**
>
> Create your own example of an "INTELIGENT" sexual opener for each one of the following three options.

Option one, STRONG INTENTION! Powerfully and directly communicate that you like, choose, and desire her!

Your example:

_____

_____

_____.

Option two, REVERSED INTENTION! Playfully act as if she's the one who desires you!

Your example:

_____

_____

_____.

71

Same Night Sex System

Option three, SOFT INTENTION! More vaguely imply sex!

Your example:

_____
_____
_____.

Step 3. Sexual Tension - How to Advance Faster by Balancing Being Forward and Laid Back!

The challenge lots of average guys encounter when going in more sexual, is that they rapidly become overwhelmingly pushy! For the most part, it's not the SEXUAL element that most women push away; it's the pushiness and excess neediness with which it is presented, which tends to create sexual repulsion. But what allows women to comfortably move forward and intensifies their interest and desire is the tension that builds when the pleasure of the option for sex is momentarily taken away!

A back and forth motion that resembles the IN and OUT rhythm followed during intercourse. I call it PRE-SEX FOREPLAY! Since it begins long before the actual sexual act takes place, as early as the very first part of the interaction. A form of mental, emotional, and even spiritual fornication that allows women to enjoy two crucial elements for them to act sexually:

1. Sexual surrender: "He wants me strong" - "IN"
2. Sexual freedom: "He won't do anything I will not want" - "OUT"

The two combined equals SEXUAL SAFETY for women. It also sub-communicates SEXUAL SELF-CONTROL on your part, and makes you stand out from the pack.

This can be done non-verbally by simply leaning back, or if you were touching her, letting go briefly. Or one of my personal favorite, the "360"! Turn around as if leaving but do a whole circle and continue the conversation. Or just release eye contact for a moment, not out of shyness, but because something else grabbed your attention.

FOR THIS TO BE NATURAL AND HAPPEN BY ITSELF, SIMPLY SHIFT YOUR CORE FOCUS FROM:

CENTERED ON HER, TO…
CENTERED ON ENJOYING YOUR OWN EXPERIENCE AROUND AND WITH HER.

The challenge for many guys is that they get so excited that a woman is finally listening and that they may at last get laid, fearing she may get away, they put all of their focus and attention on her, which creates a form of tension that is more creepy than sexual.

You can also verbally create these pauses, by saying things like… "Well anyway, I better get going before you try to seduce me…!" Or "…Don't get your hopes up, I am only briefly passing by…!" Be certain that for same night sex, just like the examples I just gave you, your verbal takeaways are done in a more teasing manner, to still serve to prime the sexual pump.

> **Example:** "I better get going before you TRY TO SEDUCE ME..." versus "I better get going my friends are waiting for me".

Step 3. Sexual Tension - How to Advance Faster by Balancing Being Forward and Laid Back!

So to build sexual tension, between each step, be certain to use these brief takeaways! They will also allow you to move forward much faster each new time that you go back in.

Another way to build sexual tension is to purposely send mixes messages. "DUAL DIRECTION ™" as I call it. If the content of what you say is more sexual, you say it more casual, and laid back. BUT NOT BORING! If the content is more casual, you say it more sexual. When telling a rather sexual story, project in your mind EASE AND FLOW. When talking non-sexual, project sexuality in your mind, for example, see her blowing you and LOVING IT.

> **Exercise: How to Advance Faster by Balancing Being Forward and Laid Back!**
>
> In front of a mirror at first, then in your interactions with women, start with a sexually charged story and say it very casually, as if talking about the most mundane thing. Be certain to lean back, and project ease in your mind, maybe even visualize a pleasant place in nature, as you talk.
>
> Then switch, go for more casual content, yet say it with a more sexual vibe and tone of voice, while in your mind, you project her riding your cock and screaming your name with pleasure!
>
> Switch back and forth a couple times, in a smooth manner that would keep the conversation flowing.
>
> Then bring it to a peak and go sexual with your words, vibe, and delivery!

Step 4: Sexual and Sub-Sexual Themes - Making ANY Topic Arousing!

Now to take it beyond the opener, and avoid falling into regular conversation, follow up with very interesting sexual and sub-sexual topics.

Sexual topics show that you don't apologize for being a man, and will arouse her, while sub-sexual topics help you bring the foundation that women need to go from arousal to action.

Since sub-sexual topics are ambiguous, they serve to bring up more sexual topics. And if you bring sexual topics first, the sub-sexual topics will then help you momentarily take it away, without going back into boring conversation, so the underneath sexual build up continues to grow. It helps to alternate between purely sexual and sub-sexual topics, to not come across as being obsessed with sex.

And by the way, it's much easier than you may think to bring up sexual themes and topics. It's really as easy as ABC.

A = Assumptions about her sexuality. "You look more like the prudish type to me!" Or "You radiate strong sexual energy, are you even aware of it?".

B = Bad mouthing other people. "OK, if we were to pair up this little guy over there with this tall chick back there, what sexual positions would you suggest they go for?"

C = Comparison between two different things and/or types. "Who do you think is capable of strongest orgasms, women in their 20s, or women in their 40s?"

D = Dare or Truth. It is childish, but works because this is how most of us were first exposed to sharing and acting on our secret desires.

Sub-sexual topics are about capturing the structure of experiences, rather than the specific experience itself. For example, instead of talking about shopping, talk about the experience of seeing something that you really want. These sub-themes are actually present in any topic. For example, I am now looking at a framed picture on the wall as I am writing this. Instead of talking about the picture itself, I could focus on how sometimes we like something so much, we want to see it again and again, so we decide to keep it where we'll be able to do that.

The basic elements to look for, for sub-sexual topics, are:

- **Desire:** What makes us want it? (IT = Whatever the topic is).
- **Action:** What makes us go for it? (IT = Whatever the topic is).
- **Pleasure:** What about it is and/or feels so good? (IT = Whatever the topic is).

- **Wanting More:** How we want to have it again? (IT = Whatever the topic is).

You can then escalate into the topic of urges, cravings, and urgency.

> **Exercise: How to Topic Chain and Escalate!**
>
> Practice picking any neutral topic, and talk about these sub-sexual elements within it. For example, if you pick "water" as a topic: "You know when you are sooo thirsty, you would do anything for a glass of water, and when you finally get it, it's like you're whole body is melting into refreshment, so good you can't help but want another round right away." To put it into practice now, simply count backwards from 3 to 1, and when you get to number 1, pick whatever is right in front of your eyes at the time as your next topic. And the only rule is to start to talk right away, and keep on talking regardless, for at least 30 seconds.

So never again can a woman stir the conversation into a boring topic, because from now on, it can ALL serve the seduction and lead to sex!

Step 5: Sexual Interest - When and How to Tell Her You Want Her!

If you don't state your interest soon, strongly, and often enough, women may put you in the friend zone. On the other hand, if you state it too early, firmly, and frequently, it may create an investment imbalance, in which she knows you're into her before you even know if she's into you. So the ideal is to find just the right balance that will neither hide it for too long, nor give it away too rapidly.

To continue to best build sexual tension and fuel her inner growing fire of desire, it helps to alternate between stating your interest and keeping her guessing. Hope and doubt, not out of cruelty, but to make sure you're not the only one making advances.

The next common mistake the average guy makes, is that he accidentally states his interest after she acted disinterested, or will act disinterested when she openly states her interest. This is confusing to women and damaging to the overall conditioning process. It also lowers his value.

Here's a very unique way to properly encourage the responses you want, and discourage the ones you don't want, while still progressing sexually.

When she is going along and supportive, state your interest directly.

Example: "Woaa, on top of being sexy, you're also talented, I like you!"

When she's hesitating, questioning, or resisting, state your interest in a reversed manner.

Example: "And just when I was starting to like you!"

Be certain to have a variety of ways to express your interest ranging from "maybe", to "most likely", all the way to "most certainly"!

Examples of Direct Statement of Interest:

"If you continue to act so sexy, I'm gonna have to kiss you!"

"Perfect, my type of girl, I like a woman who will get what she wants!"

"I like you, you're cool!"

Examples of Reversed Statement of Interest:

"Even when you screw up, you're still too cute, LOL!"

"Oh, and you were doing so well a moment ago, LOL!"

"And just when I was starting to like you, LOL!"

*Step 5: Sexual Interest -
When and How to Tell Her You Want Her!*

> **Exercise: How to Efficiently State Your Interest!**
>
> Think of a recent or imaginary interaction, and create balanced and attractive ways to express your interest.

Create your own "Direct" examples of statement of interest:

_____
_____
_____.

Create your own "Reversed" examples of statement of interest:

_____
_____
_____.

Step 6: Sexual Elicitation - Awaken the Slut Within!

Different men bring different aspects out of women. Even the most conservative girls have a "wilder side." So learn how to bring the parts of her that will best support having sex with you RIGHT NOW. Here are some extremely potent ways to do that. Keep it simple, and do it from a frame of mind of you and her just goofing and screwing around.

Part elicitation: bringing out the desired aspect through questions.

> **Example:** "When you just want to reward yourself with pleasure, what part of you comes out to play?"

Identity binding: getting her to live up to a certain identity.

> **Example:** "Most women so repress their own sexuality, but you seem more like the fully liberated Goddess type!"

85

Pretending: helping her to cut loose and reveal more since it is not for real.

> **Example:** "If you were an exotic dancer, what would be your stage name?"

Recall: getting her to experience a certain aspect of herself by remembering it.

> **Example:** "What's the wildest thing you've ever done?"

As with every question you ask women, their willingness to answer, and the quality of their answers will greatly be determined by the quality and solidity of how you ask. It helps for you to also ask yourself these questions, so they come from a more genuine place of truly being curious about such things for yourself and others, and if needed you can first provide her with your own answers as an example.

Be certain that you create conversational contexts that support such questions, avoid just asking them out of the blue, without at least saying "This may seem a bit random, but out of curiosity…!" And don't be fooled by their first answers or overly dependent on them, as sometimes, they first need to "warm up", or may not have thought of such things for a while, or ever.

Best is to also be prepared to play with them when they respond with "I don't know…!" An easy way to deal with that is to use it. I personally answer then, "Well perfect, since you don't know, I'll pick for you. As a matter a fact, I'll choose everything for you from now on. Here's what we're going to do next, we're going to walk to this quiet

Step 6: Sexual Elicitation - Awaken the Slut Within!

place over there, make-out like crazy, you're going to try to undress me, I'll say 'slow down girl...' then I'll play hard to get, until I'll finally surrender and you'll get what you want, LOL!"

"Now you were saying???"

> **Exercise: How to Bring Her Wild Side Out!**
>
> To get her to talk about and connect with the more adventurous and playful aspect of herself, be certain to first be more connected with this part of you as well. Start to practice bringing up such questions in your interactions. Be flexible and customize them as needed.

Based on the given examples, create your own example for each of the elicitation techniques listed.

1. Part elicitation: Formula, "When you just want to_____ _____, what part of you comes out?"

Create your own example:

_____
_____
_____.

2. Identity binding: Formula, "Most women are so_____ _____, but you seem more like_____!"

Same Night Sex System

Create your own example:

_____
_____
_____.

3. Pretending: Formula, "If you were_____,
what would be your _____?"

Create your own example:

_____
_____
_____.

4. Recall: Formula, "What's the _____
thing you've ever done?"

Create your own example:

_____
_____
_____.

Step 7: Sequential Seduction - Secrets of Sexual Conditioning!

The gap between DESIRE and "DOING IT" has to be bridged in increments. Ultimately, it's a process of conditioning in which small steps lead to bigger steps. I refer to this as "SEQUENTIAL SEDUCTION ™". Not only you are conditioning the individual steps, you are also conditioning TAKING STEPS. Because in the end, at the level of what it will take for her to go for it, the mechanics are rather similar whether it is to hug, high five, or hump!

So here's an extremely potent and truly "female friendly" way to assist a woman to go from arousal to action, the way only a truly experienced modern day Casanova would. Women long for assistance at that level, since unlike us; they don't necessarily put arousal and action in the same bucket.

The "Arousal Into Action" Model!

This model includes all the basic and more advanced elements of attraction, comfort, and seduction needed. It is designed to physically escalate regardless, and will create incredible sexual tension.

1. Warn Her! Use whatever she's doing as what will be the cause for your actions. So she's responsible for them.

> **Example:** "If you continue to look at me in this sexy way, I am going to kiss you!"

It may help to also disassociate, by giving her lips a life of their own. Example: "Better tell your lips to stop desiring me...."

Note: As with Reversed Statements of Interest, even if her answers and behavior appear counter productive, you can still use what she offers. For example, as a reply to her saying that she can't stay, you could say something like, "I must warn you, if you continue to say no in such a cute shy way, I'll have to hug you for it, LOL!"

2. Act On It! Dominantly do it! Without saying anything, seize the moment while she's still laughing and probably trying to explain that she wasn't.

3. Playfully Punish Her! Even if she resisted, you further escalate physically by blaming her for it.

If she went along, tell her: "So you think you can just seduce me like that...LOL" then do it again!

If she didn't, tell her: "Bad girl!!! Trying to seduce me, I warned you...LOL" Spank her playfully.

This is done as a way to "lubricate" the interaction and make it easier for both you and her to comfortably escalate. On your side, it helps you not to hesitate since the humor and playfulness diffuse the over-investment that she may

Step 7: Sequential Seduction - Secrets of Sexual Conditioning!

not go for it, and on her side, it gives her the permission to feel comfortable. That is why this model is so extremely potent. You must experiment with it.

That's the basic part, now on to the advanced part.

4. Bind Her! Make the original thing you warned her NOT to do, a sign of superiority, a plus, and compliment her for it.

> **Example:** "But you know, it takes a powerful woman, to act like you want to be kissed."

5. Comfort and Genuine Interest! Ground the experience to make her feel safe and show a different aspect of you, by naturally deepening your voice, grabbing her hand, and making her feel safe as you say something like, "You're fun, I like you."

6. Direct and Take her! Lead her to the next spot, and part of the adventure. Simply take her by the hand and say: "Come on, let's go over there, it be fun..."

> **Exercise: How to Turn Arousal Into ACTION!**
>
> There are so many ways and opportunities to use this model and the mindset that supports it. So start to experiment with your own ideas to apply it to hug, touch, kiss, relocate, and sexually escalate rapidly.

Same Night Sex System

Write down your own example for each step.

1. Warn her! "If you continue to look at me in this sexy way, I am going to kiss you".

Now create your own example:

_____

_____

_____.

2. Act on it! Dominantly do it!

Simply imagine yourself going for it, and allow your body to relax as you SEE YOURSELF DOING IT. The more often your mind rehearses it, the easier it becomes to DO IT IN REAL SITUATIONS.

3. Playfully punish her! "So you think you can just seduce me like that...LOL" Spank her playfully.

Now create your own example:

_____

_____

_____.

Step 7: Sequential Seduction - Secrets of Sexual Conditioning!

4. Bind Her! "But you know, it takes a powerful woman, to act like you want to be kissed."

Now create your own example:

_____
_____
_____.

5. Comfort and Genuine Interest! Ground the experience to make her feel safe and show a different aspect of you, by deepening your voice, grabbing her hand, and making her feel safe by saying something like: "You're fun, I like you."

Now create your own example:

_____
_____
_____.

6. Direct and Take her! Lead her to the next spot, and part of the adventure. Simply take her by the hand and say: "Come on, let's go over there, it'll be fun..."

Now create your own example:

_____
_____
_____.

Sexual Surrender - When to Shut Up and Take Her!

As independent as women may say they have become, whether it is by nature or the result of thousands of years of conditioning, they'll still tend to wait for you to be the one sexually initiating, in most situations.

On the other hand, many men tend to keep on trying to "talk her" into it, when they should "take her" into it. This is same night sex's final frontier that will separate the men from the boys.

So on one side you SURRENDER and LET IT HAPPEN by quieting your mind and easing up your body. And on the other side, you MAKE IT happen, by taking her with no apology to sweep her off her feet. This is the perfect blend between the female and male energy that is within all of us. If you resist or hesitate at either of these levels yourself, she's likely to match and duplicate it, so know when to just...SHUT UP AND TAKE HER.

NMS = Next Morning SEX!

Finally, the next best thing to SAME NIGHT SEX is NEXT MORNING SEX! There's times when perhaps because relocating to sexual location took too long and she's falling asleep, or gets a headache, or in the event she puts up more resistance than expected, and all attempts seem to lead nowhere, then best is to let it simmer until morning, and start fresh then.

BUT NEVER AS AN EXCUSE ON YOUR PART!

Next Morning Sex Strategies:

If it really seems that she's not going to go for it that same night, at least secure sleeping in the same bed! Be certain to give a restriction, such as "Ok, we can cuddle, but promise me, NO SEX". Then enjoy a brief moment of light cuddling and caressing, until you take it away and turn your back on her to go to sleep. After a night next to your warm body, with you NOT being pushy about it, she'll much more easily go for it in the morning.

Same Night Sex System

Again, never use this option out of fear to escalate, or because you're buying into her friendship frame, only use this as a smart last resort.

And then the next morning...

1. Be certain that you are up before her, so just in case you don't wake up alone in bed, or she's already dressed and ready to go. Do whatever it takes, best is to preprogram your phone alarm with a light tone, and keep it right next to you.

2. Right away, the moment she opens her eyes, initiate playfulness by accusing her of having been all over you during her sleep. Wrestle and spank her for it.

3. Re-escalate from there, since when just waking up, we are much more suggestible to what is presented. Lead into more games, perhaps a little massage, anything that gets it going physically. You can simply bring what best worked the prior night back.

Best is to make sure you and her stay in the bed. In case she gets up you can always do it in the shower, or on kitchen floor!

And in the worst case, if she really doesn't want to, since THERE'S PLENTY for you out there, you can either use the same techniques to reschedule, or simply let it go, and be grateful for the learning experience and fun time together.

The ones that don't go for it are really there to help you refine your approach and propel you towards the ones that will!

✴ Conclusion ✴

Sexual Synchronicity - The Invisible Magical Ingredient!

In my own days of "dating desperation" wondering why I wasn't getting anywhere or why it was taking so long, busy blaming women or even myself for my shortcomings, I blindly was overlooking the basic following facts:

1. How soon was I giving up?

The answer basically was "even before I really began," LOL! Too often I left interactions with women or even got upset at them ASSuming too early that it wasn't working!

2. What meaning did I attach to women's responses?

My lack of trust in myself often caused me to give the worst meaning to whatever women said or did, taking it all way too personally!

3. What habits was I conditioning?

Without realizing it, even though I was taking more steps, I was also piling up more emotional baggage!

Fortunately, through time, I started to embrace a whole new paradigm, which lead me all the way to true core sexual satisfaction and much more, with so much gratification, and wonderful learning opportunities along the way.

What started to change is that I started to recognize the mysterious ways in which with the right attitude, nothing ever goes wrong. One woman leads to another, a no show gets you at the right place to meet a woman who is more ready. The "Nos" lead to the "Yeses"! The one who resists is really there to help you refine your approach. Even the inner feelings that used to bother you now seem to serve you. Any anxiety is really there to lead you towards confidence! Disappointment opens the door to deeper decisions and real resolutions to use it all to do well...!

So in conclusion, to put it in simple words: Whether you already did get some fun sexual adventures or not, is absolutely irrelevant!!! Why???

Because as we said many times throughout this book, every guy out there wants and NEEDS to get laid, and when they don't they get upset, discouraged, and lose their enthusiasm and confidence and eventually give up, or settle for less than they could have.

So what is that secret gold nugget that makes all the difference?

When you recognize what most consider "the end," as "the beginning", you open the door to an infinite array of incredible fun, fulfillment and satisfaction in not only your sex and love life, in ALL aspects of your life! It's beyond persistence, it's about tuning into that gentle breeze -- so to speak, that leads you exactly where you need to be, like following a river all the way to the ocean.

I know, this sounds all poetic and kind of spiritual, but there's a reason we call guys who do very well with women by default "naturals." Perhaps it also refers to the fact that when you trust the natural progression and suspend for a moment the "average way" to look at an interaction with a woman that didn't go anywhere. Refrain from blaming or judging her, yourself, women or the process, and stay open to the possibility that maybe there was a true gift there...

And instead of letting your energy and enthusiasm cave in and succumb to what seemed like a failure at first, recognize the opportunity. Maybe that girl gave you a chance to fine-tune, practice or even to learn how to sustain your faith in yourself regardless of what women may think. Perhaps she was there to lead you to another woman nearby. Since we just don't know, why not assume the best that could serve us?

I personally opt, as silly as it may seem to some, for the possibility that maybe there is an interconnection between all women on the planet in which they guide us men towards the ones amongst them who will most appreciate and enjoy us. An ultimate win/win in which both men and women get to grow. A form of reversed paranoia, in which instead of thinking that women are out there to get you, realize they are out there to help you!

And of course, this applies to your learning as well. There too, let what most would consider the end or a problem be the beginning and an invitation to solutions. So, re-read, and complete the exercises you haven't yet or re-do them, as in the end, your success is up to you and only depends on your ability to apply the following "Magic Words"...

GO UNTIL!

The real distraction and obstacle is not "the girlfriend who tries to pull her away" or the "the guy that's trying to hijack the conversation", it is simply our lack

of resilience and ability to readjust as needed, UNTIL!

The good news is that you can CHANGE THAT STARTING NOW!

Thank you for the opportunity to be of assistance. Be good to yourself and to all the beautiful women who'll get to enjoy your new, powerful, and irresistible true sexual and romantic self!

Vince Kelvin

Your BONUS Complimentary Training

1. Your FREE Invite to Global Pickup/Seduction List!

Get daily tips, feedback, and ask questions!

Go to:

www.groups.yahoo.com/group/Self-Empowermentgroup/

Or register at www.SeductionCoaching.com

2. Participate in The FREE Global PUA Conference Call!

Every Monday, 7pm PST!

Call **(712) 432-1100 then enter 721797#**

Your opportunity to talk directly to Vince and ask him any question you may have! FOR FREE!!!

www.SeductionCoaching.com

www.PUASummit.com

THOTH/ROCHELLE
Publications

UPGRADE TODAY AND GET THE 5 CD SET!

- Want to feel sufficiently sexually attractive to bed 10s and beyond?

- Wish gorgeous girls would think of you as the sexual stud they crave?

Then, if you are daring enough to get to the core of your sexuality and start to...**See Yourself As The Sexual Man Hot Women Have to Have...**

THE SAME NIGHT SEX HOME STUDY COURSE!

CD 1: Same Night Sex MINDSET
- Properly Set Sexual Structure from the Start!

CD 2: Same Night Sex MECHANICS
- Accelerate Her Arousal Until She Will ACT ON IT!

CD 3: Sexual Identity Shaping (TM) MIND-PROGRAMMING
- Break FREE from Past Sexual Insecurities!

Bonus CD: Sex-Appeal Strengthening (TM) MEDITATION
- BE The Highly Sexual Man Women Crave!

- **Gift CD: Action Plan To MAKE IT HAPPEN**

UPGRADE NOW for **just $96.75**, normally $129!

To order on line: www.SeductionCoaching.com, then ENTER the coupon code: **UPGRADE** for your 25% off discount during checkout!
Via email: Vince@SeductionCoaching.com
By phone: (323) 309-3219, toll free 1-866-96-HYPNO (49766)

THE ANNUAL PICKUP ACADEMY
One Week Lifestyle Mastery Training!

Located In Beautiful "Babe Packed" Sunny Santa Monica California!

Experience a COMPLETE MANHOOD MAKE OVER!!!

Your Whole Week of Training with Vince Includes:

- **DAILY MORNING INNER GAME MASTERY SESSION, AT THE BEACH!!!**
Using Meditation, Self-Hypnosis, Ritual Magic, NLP, and Vince's Core Intention Technology (C.I.T.)!

- **EMBODYING THE FOUR VIBES AND ARCHETYPES OF THE MULTI-DIMENSIONAL MAN!**
Focusing on one vibe per day for the first four days, then on combining them!

- **DAILY ONE HOUR DELIVERY AND IMPROVISATION DRILLS!!!**
Full conversational continuity workouts, and complete body language, tonality and volume tune up!

- **DAILY "IN FIELD" INTENSIVE COACHING AND MENTORING!!!**
Building one step at a time, focusing on one phase of pickup process per day!

- **Bonus private IMAGE make-over consultation, and fitness evaluation!**

- And fun time by the "babe packed" pool and jacuzzi, and ocean. Including a special **SOCIAL CIRCLE** barbecue and pool party for which you'll get to invite all the girls you'll have met during the week!

PLUS DAILY 2 HOUR CLASS TOPICS:

Monday:	APPROACH MASTERY!
Tuesday:	NUMBER CLOSING AND PHONE GAME MASTERY!
Wednesday:	INSTA-DATE AND DAY 2 MASTERY
Thursday:	R&R AND BEACH PICKUP!
Friday:	NIGHT GAME MASTERY!
Saturday:	LTRs MASTERY!
Sunday:	LIFESTYLE MASTERY, and Graduation Ceremony!

With Vince and the team! Plus a surprise handful of special guests such as:
David Wygant, Marni from the Wing Girl Method, Adam Lyons, Speer, Sexual Chocolate, Hydro, Asian Playboy, and Yoga and Fitness Trainers!

LIMITED TO ONLY 10 PARTICIPANTS,
Second Week of July, Yearly!

For more information go to www.SeductionCoaching.com
or call Toll Free 1-866-96-HYPNO (49766), direct (323) 309-3219

✷ About the Author ✷

European born and now Los Angeles based founder of SeductionCoaching.com, **Vince Kelvin** started his wild journey to wisdom with women in the early 90s.

After over two decades of assisting people to take charge of all aspects of their lives, he brings to the pickup community a truly unique, holistic, and efficient angle!

His track record of over 17000 hours of private sessions and having addressed over 2500 audiences worldwide, have resulted into a very genuine, practical, and simple approach to a truly fulfilling and fun social, sex, and love life!

Vince is now happily married to **Amy M. Kelvin**. Together they produce the yearly **Original PUA World Summit in Hollywood.**

To contact Vince via email:
Vince@SeductionCoaching.com
Twitter:
http://twitter.com/1VinceKelvin
Facebook:
http://www.facebook.com/vincekelvin?ref=profile

www.ingramcontent.com/pod-product-compliance
Lightning Source LLC
Chambersburg PA
CBHW050650160426
43194CB00010B/1881